Waiting for the Dawn

Poetry from the depths to the light

by

Maggie Shaw

Waiting for the Dawn

Poetry from the depths
to the light

by

Maggie Shaw

eregendal.com

Also by the Author:
The Vision and Beyond (2018)
Diviner's Nemesis I – Avenger (2019)
Diviner's Nemesis II – Retribution (2020)
The Eagle and The Butterfly (2020)
The Last Thursday Ritual in Little Piddlington (2021)
The Eagle and The Raven (2021)

First published in the United Kingdom in 2022 by
Eregendal.com, Rosehill Road, Crewe, Cheshire CW2 8AR.
Printed in the United Kingdom by Lulu.com.

ISBN 978-1-8381313-2-6 (paperback)

Contents

Introduction and Acknowledgements

Waiting for the Dawn: Poetry from the depths to the light is a collection of poems and songs I wrote over the course of my life. The poems fell naturally into seven broad groups as I collated the collection.

The poems chart my progress through life. The earliest poems were written when I was a teenage runaway in London. My most prolific period followed my return through to years of treatment for clinical depression. I wrote less poetry after 1984, as I found a different way to live through the 12-Step Program. More recently, following a late diagnosis of Autistic Spectrum Disorder, I entered a wonderful third-age period of creativity and contentment. The poems are not in chronological order, though. Recovery, as someone once told me, is not a straight diagonal line on the graph of life, from zero to 100%. Rather, it happens in a series of waves, with each peak usually a little higher than the previous one, and each dip usually not so deep.

Many people have helped me through the different stages of life: my years of depression, addiction, recovery, diagnosis, education and publishing. I try to repay my debt to them by supporting others in the way they generously supported me.

I would like to thank those who helped with this book in any way. Roy Butler gave me invaluable guidance with the manuscript. Eregendal's social media followers Linda Keser and Claudia East won the competitions to choose the title and cover design. Special thanks go to Eglė Rakauskaitė, the daughter of the late Lithuanian photographer Romualdas Rakauskas, for giving me permission to include her father's photograph *Flowering*, on page 106. All other images were supplied by www.canva.com, apart from my own photos on pages 46 and 72, and the Clan MacThomas Society's badge on page 102.

As always, any faults in the book are my own alone.

Section One

Love

The evocative poem *Into Grey* seems to make no sense at first: for how can sunshine make the world grey? The metaphor is a device to describe the transforming power of love at first sight. The beloved is so arresting to the senses that the world around turns to a monochrome background in their transcending full-colour presence.

Into Grey   **13th July 1975**

Sunshine tinge the world with grey –
I see you on that sunlit day,
But the image is in black and white:
Bright colour faded in your light.

Debased to monochrome were we,
Transient in infinity;
And yet we knew that we could be
What we thought that we could see.

So light and night did not dismay,
Though when I saw you on that day
The laws of light were disobeyed
And colour faded into grey.

The wistful song *A Little Love Song* describes the innocent romantic dream of a sixteen-year-old teenager: creating a little island in the sun for her beloved to sail her to.

A Little Love Song   1971

I have a little love song for you
Which I hope you'll listen to.

I'd go out when the sun rose in the east,
And catch it in a jam jar,
And bring it home to you.

I have a little sunshine for you,
Which I hope will brighten you.

I'd walk along the seashore at low tide
And pick up every pebble
And put it in the sea.

I have a little island for you
Which I hope you will go to.

I'd tie up every north wind in a sail,
Which I'd tie upon a mast
Upon a wooden yacht.

I have a little sail boat for you
Which I hope won't fail you.

And you could sail me to that island
And we'd tie up on a tree
While the bright sun blazed down.

I have a little day dream for you
Which I hope you'll come into.

The song *Wednesday Morning* describes the author's move from London to West Cumberland with her first husband in 1973. After their wedding they struggled to find a place to set up home in or around London. Instead, they moved north to West Cumberland, the place Maggie loved most, in the Lake District where her father's family had farmed for generations.

Wednesday Morning 1973

It's Wednesday morning,
Time to get up out of bed;
So rise and shine dear:
There's a brand new day ahead.
There's a new world waiting for us,
So come on, rise and shine.
The dawn's gone, birds are singing -
There's so much to do, but the day is yours and mine.

It's Wednesday morning
And the sun is shining down;
So let's get out dear,
Before the world spins too far round.
It's the first day that we've been so
Far from the city's streets and towers.
Out in the country we'll have to fight hard,
But what we get, we'll know is ours.

It's Wednesday morning:
Dawns the first day that we're free.
So wear your jeans dear,
We've escaped that vast city.
No-one to hurt us, or to do us down -
We've only nature with which to fight,
And as we try to build our own new world,
We'll know that what we did was really right.

It's Wednesday morning -
We've got so much to see and do.
But you can smile, dear,
'Cause I'm so glad that I've got you.
Yes, you can smile dear,
Because together we'll see it through.

The sad poem *Reassurance* marks the start of a relationship going wrong. But why is the reassurance needed? Looking back, it is clear it would have been better to have discussed the problem in addition to writing the poem. Too often, we expect people to know intuitively what we are thinking and to respond as we would like. But how can a person really know what is wrong, if we do not tell them?

Reassurance

Tell me that you love me –
No, don't try to turn away.
I know you show me in your deeds,
But I want to hear you say.

Tell me that you want me.
No, don't look the other way.
I know you want me by your side,
But I want to hear you say.

Tell me that you need me.
No, don't smile and glance away.
I know you need me in your life,
But I want to hear you say.

Tell me that I am your life
And without me you'd not last a day.
I know you prove it with your deeds,
But I want to hear you say.

Tell me that I am your queen,
Without me skies are always grey.
I know you think it in your heart,
But I want to hear you say.

Tell me, love: I want to hear.
Why do you turn away?
Why don't you ease my heavy heart?
Why can't you say?

The title of the poem, *Heartbreak Hotel (revisited)* refers to the song made famous by Elvis Presley, but has little else in common with his big hit. Depression and the learned habit of keeping emotions to ourselves, can cause creeping damage to relationships. This poem forecasts what will happen two years later, and reveals the poet's lack of emotional maturity to prevent it even though she can see it coming.

Heartbreak Hotel (revisited)   25th February 1975

You stand in the foyer of Heartbreak Hotel,
An unpopular place which many know well.
You don't yet know how it is done up inside,
Or even that that's where you're going to reside.

The foyer tells nothing of what is upstairs:
The concierge smiles kindly with a distant air.
With a last hopeful look, you glance back at me,
And with a sad smile, I describe what you'll see.

Your comfortable room is cold, grey and dark.
The night is oppressive, but light makes it stark.
Your bed is well slept in, and relaxing too,
But when you are in it, no sleep comes to you.

The corridors may seem so empty and bare,
But the carpets are worn and thin on the stair.
If you go to the lounge, you will find it filled,
But no-one will speak for they all have your ill…

I'm sorry, my love, I should drive you to here.
I can't say any more, though I see it clear.
I made a mistake on a route I know well,
And once more brought someone to Heartbreak Hotel.

All You Left was written as a song that told a story. Vestiges of the story turn up in the author's *Zoe Manson* series of novels, at present awaiting a publication date.

The abandoned lover reflects on what has been left after their beloved has gone. In the novel, it was Zoe who had left, leaving her husband with the baby and the ring.

All you left   **Spring 1971**

All you left me was a ring
And a note
Telling me
It was all off.

All you left me was a hope
Or a prayer
Asking God
To bring you back.

All you left me was a star
To wish on…
Wishing you
Were back here now.

All you left me was a son
Who'll grow up
Seeking you
To ask you home.

Come Home was written while the author was a teenage runaway in London. Once she had overcome the suicidal emotions that had forced her departure, she reflected on her situation as she imagined what her parents' point of view would be.

Her mental health had improved in the two years she lived as a runaway in London, but degenerated again after her return at the age of seventeen. Fifty years later, the reason for this became clear when she was diagnosed with Autistic Spectrum Disorder. The mishandling of her neurodivergent personality by her parents and school had happened through no fault of their own. Autism in high functioning females was not recognised to be an issue for another thirty years.

Come Home Winter 1970-71

Ghost town train's gonna take me away.
What d'ya say?
Take me to the shore:
Won't see you no more.
Come home.

Conscience may not kill me here,
But I fear
That you won't come back,
Though even calls the rock,
Come home.

Loneliness is the last place I want you to be.
Come back to me!
Fly with the curlew,
Like my words flew…
Come home.

Escape was difficult when I made you chained:
Your nature strained;
So though the beck prays,
You'll never stay.
Come home.

Why waste words and space?
You've no face
To return.
You'll learn.
Come home.

23

For You   **14th March 1975**

Dreaming memories,
Memories of summer,
Of another;
But the melody's for you.

Dreaming wishes,
Wishes of springtime,
Of sunshine;
But the melody's for you.

Singing melodies,
Melodies of laughter,
Melodies of beauty;
Melodies of you.

Singing melodies,
Melodies of springtime,
Melodies of summer:
Melodies of you.

Song of the Seasons   September 1973

I first saw you in the spring time:
As the sun glowed down
We sat beneath the trees
And drank the wine;
And the hillside decked with nature's gown of green:
'Twas so serene –
How I'd love to leap the years and have you by me.

I first loved you in the summer:
As the flowers bloomed
We sat beside the sea
To watch the colours
Of the sunlight through the water's silver glow:
My heart flowed –
How I'd love to leap the years and have you by me.

I first hurt you in the autumn:
As the leaves fell down,
Painting the pavements red;
Those things I said
Weren't meant to cut you like I'd stabbed you with a sword:
Those cruel words!
How I'd love to leap the years and have you by me.

I last saw you in the winter:
As your train pulled out
I hid the tears I cried,
Just waved goodbye:
And the fog came down and hid you from my eyes:
Our last goodbye –
How I'd love to leap the years and have you by me.

Section Two

Life

The reflection *My Life,* about the author's life as a teenage runaway in London is not what one might expect. She found safety and security through having a job, attending church regularly and living in a flat shared with four other young women. Not every runaway becomes a delinquent.

My Life

Waiting, waiting,
Always waiting:
What am I waiting for?

Talking, talking,
Always talking:
What am I talking about?

Working, working,
Always working:
What am I working towards?

Hoping, hoping,
Always hoping:
What am I hoping to gain?

Travelling, travelling,
Always travelling:
Where am I travelling to?

Searching, searching,
Always searching:
What am I searching for?

My Life is like a Long-Distance Train is an extended metaphor, based on a journey the poet had made two years earlier in 1971. It was written shortly before she married for the first time. Because of her autism, her understanding of the continuity of relationships differs from most people's. She found it easier than others do to drop out of a relationship when circumstances move on, as reflected in this observation.

My Life is like a Long-Distance Train   Spring 1973

My life is like a long-distance train
That I boarded in a hurry when born,
Getting on at the very back.

The people on the train are all the people I will meet.
Some I sit with for a while. Then leave.
Others join me in my travels
As I move to the front of the train, and death.
Others chase after me once I've passed.
But most I don't notice, and they don't notice me.

There is no use in moving back down the train:
My last stop, I must get out at the front.
But I don't know how long the train is,
Nor do any of the passengers
Apart from perhaps one or two.
For having boarded in a hurry,
We omitted to look.

Uncertainty describes a day when the autistic poet struggled to understand what was going on with those around her. Spectrum people often take time to mentally process events and understand them. This poem is about a time when that processing had only just started.

Uncertainty

Today was an odd day:
A lot of things happened,
That didn't happen;
A lot of things were said,
That weren't said –
Aye, today was an odd day.

Today was a weird day:
A lot of things were done,
As weren't done;
A lot of things were seen,
As weren't seen:
Aye, today was a weird day.

A reassuring comment from a friend
Who wasn't a friend,
Which brought up some fears in the heart
Which weren't fears,
And set the mind to dreaming
Yet not dreaming,
Because logic knew...
And yet did not know.

Aye, today was an odd day.
But this much I do know:
That what happened, what was said, done, and seen
Was a lot further from the truth than
That which was not said, done or seen; did not happen –
Aye, today was an odd day.

Hunter describes the poet's search for understanding about life as a teenager. It is one of her circular poems in structure, implying that the answer has not yet been found.

Where will you take me, O Ship?
Can you take me to be free?
  I can only show you foreign lands
  And a watery grave in the sea.

Where will you take me, O Man?
Can you take me to be free?
  I can only show you hate and love,
  And an imperfect mind and body.

Where will you take me, O Money?
Will you take me to be free?
  I can only show you a life of greed,
  With worried nights, locked doors and enmity.

Where will you take me, O Car?
Can you take me to be free?
  I can only show you endless roads,
  A never-ending destiny.

Where will you take me, O Death?
Will you take me to be free?
  I can only show you the grave
  And then you're done with me.

Where will you take me, O Bible?
Will you take me to be free?
  I'll take you to heaven if you obey
  From now till eternity.

Where will you take me, O Ship?
Will you take me to be free…?

Habit

Smoke wreath
Circle
Up to heaven
Fly, windwards.

Hundreds
Daily
Up to heaven
So peaceful.

Flower wreath
White stone
Up to heaven
The end.

Ageing Day   13th November 1972

Ageing day,
Your darkness chokes me
Like pollution in the city.

Ageing day,
Your stillness deafens me
Like traffic in the city.

Ageing day,
Your loneliness stifles me,
Like bedsits in the city.

Ageing day,
Your emptiness worries me,
Like people in the city.

Ageing day,
Your shortness amazed me,
Like friendship in the city.

Dead day,
Your life passed me
Like a cigarette
In the city.

The End

And it died.
Yet they laughed and danced –
They were at a party:
They didn't give it a second glance,
Nor did they think of me;
So it died.

And you sighed.
Yet they drank and joked –
They were in a good scene:
They didn't think of us other folk,
Nor did they see what had been;
So you sighed.

And I... well, I cried.
Yet they grinned and sang –
They were having a good time:
They didn't listen as the bell rang,
Nor did they hear the last chime;
So I cried.

And Satan lied.
Yet they danced with him –
They were living their life;
They didn't bother about their sin,
Nor did they care for strife;
So Satan lied.

And Man shied,
Yet they led him on –
They were having their fun:

They didn't care that he was all alone,
Nor did they think they'd lose the Son;
So Man shied.

And God tried.
Yet they had not changed –
They were enjoying mortality;
They didn't realise things could end up so strange.
Nor did you and I, though – neither did we.
So God tried.

And creation died.

This sad poem describes the self-centredness of many people in the face of social issues and natural disasters. For decades, those whose wealth and social standing benefitted from the status quo, ridiculed people who expressed concern about the damage being done to the planet. How poignant that seems now, nearly fifty years later, as more and more countries find their weather reaching dangerous extremes and their homes and livelihoods threatened through climate change.

Winning 25th September 1972

Winning 25th **September 1972**

The day has come.
The happy people meet in the street,
And greet the sun.

The day has come.
Laughter abounds all around.
The town is one.

The day has come.
The citizens shout: no doubt is about,
Just fun.

The day has come.
Festivity, not enmity, is all we see
Around.

The day has come, the day has come.
For we have won,
And home we run.
The day has come. The day has come!

Thoughts on Remembrance Sunday 13th November 1977

Now they sleep,
They who warred with nations.
They rest in foreign lands,
They who raised our banner
From the ashes of their regiments;
They who summoned courage
From the depths of hearts like yours and mine:
Aye, now they sleep.

And we live on
In the world they fought for.
But is ours the peace that they foresaw?
They who laid their lives
On the altar of Mars –
Is he placated now?

Our swords are hung on the wall,
But our neighbours' swords are drawn:
We hear the grind of steal 'gainst stone;
In the distance drums are beating,
And the trumpet calls plaintively.

I shed some tears for those who died,
For theirs was a noble sacrifice;
But then I moved on.
There is a time for all things;
The few tears for their memory are just –
I shed many tears for this present.
Is this what they fought for?
And died?

A Heart So Set voices the teenage struggle to make sense of life. When introspection is not drowned out by busy living, the young adult mind can find the world with its opportunities confusing. This commentary on politics and society is still as relevant today as it was when it was written nearly fifty years ago.

A heart So Set   4th October 1974

A heart so set...
Searching in the dark for an answer to the clues;
Finding in the dark only another question.

A heart so set –
Looking through the speeches for a truth to explain;
Seeing in the speeches only another lie.

A heart so set -
Listening in the silence for a sound to hear;
Finding in the silence only another silence.

A heart so set -
Asking all the people for a way to succeed;
Listening to all the people to learn only how to lose.

Will that question be answered?
Will that lie be retracted?
Will that silence be broken?
Will that loss be regained?

A heart so set
Will doubt not through the maze,
Though lost and aimless appears the path,
Though barren and stony is the world around.

A heart so set
Can only succeed,
Or drop at the last, still fighting.

Section Three

Depression

If the poems in this section speak so deeply to you that they take you back into the deep mineshaft of depression, please try to seek help. Lives can be transformed, just as the poet's life eventually was, through the help of supportive, non-judgemental people.

Portrait of the author at Regents Park Zoo, winter 1970-71
taken by a friend

Epitaph was written as the poet's pen portrait of herself in her mid-teens. The image the world saw of a bright, eccentric persona vanished into darkness when she was alone. This is typical of autistic masking. The poem is also a song, with an eerie, haunting tune which is difficult to sing.

Epitaph August 1971

In the day
She wore sun in her hair;
But at night
She wore black.

In the day
She wore the sky as her cloak;
But at night
She wore black.

In the day
She wore garlands of flowers;
But at night
She wore black.

In the day
She wore the day;
But at night
She wore black.

The Load was written while the poet was living as a teenage runaway in London. In retrospect, she was clearly trying to process the problems of being autistic in a neurotypical world, almost fifty years before she was finally diagnosed as being on the spectrum.

The poem gained a bluesy song tune, and was recorded for release on World Mental Health Day in 2021.

The Load January 1971

It's a long road,
it's a heavy load,
it's a tiresome goad,
It sure is a heavy load.
And I can't go no further, cos it's a heavy load,
No, I can't go no further cos it's a heavy load.

It's a different way,
it's a stormy day,
and it's nice to lay me down,
Cos I sure have a heavy load.
And I can't go no further, cos it's a heavy load,
No, I can't go no further cos it's a heavy load.

It's a stony path,
through their cruel laugh,
and their bitter wrath:
Aye, it sure is a heavy load.
And I can't go no further, cos it's a heavy load,
No, I can't go no further cos it's a heavy load.

It's a mean life
full of bitter strife,
endless lonely grief,
as I sure have a heavy load.
And I can't go no further, cos it's a heavy load,
No, I can't go no further cos it's a heavy load.

Goodbye is an unusual poem which uses stream-of-consciousness writing to describe the chaotic mental processes ruling the poet's head during a time of intense depression.

Stream-of-consciousness writing can be therapeutic and revealing. Start with a pen and a blank sheet of paper, or a new Word document, and write or type whatever comes to mind, without going back to censure or edit. When words have finally run out, finish the piece and read back what is on the page.

Goodbye 10th September 1974

Goodbye 10th September 1974

I laughed
You cried
He sneered
She smiled

I sighed
They lied

Two seventeen the train came in
The rain came in
We sat in the café
Unhappy

Grey sugar plum dangled on my cheek front
Across the midnight star shine pomegranate's
Sullen shadow of stupid suntan strip.
I knew their answer wasn't right –
You can't phase three with two with one with me
They said I was okay
But it wasn't the case when they left me.
Those burnt images can't really know,
The fools, but I don't want to bother
Cos it's not worth star shine on the window
It's worth no more than suntan strip
To set the juicy jewels on the bum King's thorny crown
So sit there and worship him, you crazy fools
Cos that's all you can think of now

Now that the bottom's fallen out of the world
And there's distance between the he and the she
Was it them, or is it you and me?
Images like rain fall on the sodden ground
I look, but I'm the only one around.

Depression 29th April 1975

Oh, that this day of days
Into endless night could pass
Away;
And that this hour of hours
The laws of timelessness
Obey.

Oh, that this yearning emptiness
Could like some sombre phantom of the night
Be laid,
And that these unfulfilled desires
Could drift like wind-blown wreaths of mist
And fade.

Oh, that this aching soul
Like some hushed breeze could cease
To sigh;
And that this tired heart
Could fade like winter flowers
And die.

Oh, that these uncried tears
Could turn to river torrents
And flow;
And that this worthless flesh
Beneath the cold dark earth
Could go.

Revisited 23rd June 1975

I am living in a mineshaft of man-made griefs
Where silence reigns and nothing breathes,
And darkness obscures all those tawdry beliefs –
What price light for night?

I am drifting in a pattern of chaotic hell
Where infinity cries with the tale it tells,
And darkness cocoons me in a fatal shell –
What price light for night?

I am encaged in a prison of searing hate
Where malice breeds and depression bates
The darkness with barbed shafts of cold, crushing fate –
What price light for night?

I am running in a rat race of convention's form
Where regrets point cold fingers at my inadequate norm,
And darkness prevents me from riding the storm.
What price light for night?

I am fleeing the great tidal wave at my lowest ebb,
I am running the storm of fear and dread,
In the darkness that cuts my mind's eye from my head –
What price light for night?

I am drowning in failure's merciless waves:
Pierced and held down by despair's leaden staves,
While darkness leaves me with no hope to be saved.
What price light for night?

To Those who Make People Fit for Society

23rd September 1974

They took my body and filled it full of drugs
They stretched it and boiled it
They squeezed it and coiled it
And I don't think it'll work any more.

They took my heart and filled it full of hate
They stuffed it and cut it
They stabbed it and hurt it
And I don't think it'll love any more.

They took my mind and filled it full of lies
They starved it and froze it
They stripped and re-clothed it
And I don't think it'll know any more.

They took my soul and filled it full of fear
They spiked it and battered it
They struck it and bedevilled it
And I don't think it'll believe any more.

They took my eyes and blinded them
They took my ears and deafened them
They took my desires and played on them
They took my truths and twisted them.

They took my laughter and silenced it
They took my life and killed it
They took my love and stifled it
They took my route and obscured it.

They took my brother and destroyed him
They took my lover and denied him
They took my devil and worshipped him
They took my God and crucified him.

They took my philosophy and filled it full of death
They screwed it and bent it
They scattered it and rent it
And I don't think it will ever help again.

They took my pride and flattened it
They took my trust and betrayed it
They took my honour and distorted it
They took my cause and ridiculed it.

They took me and they filled me full of them
They disregarded me, tried to change me,
Couldn't rearrange, so they discarded me
And I don't think I can ever face their world again.

This sad poem describes the writer's grief at the process used to turn her autistic behaviours into those of a neurotypical person. It details just how destructive the process was, and why it caused her recurring bouts of clinical suicidal depression.

The poet uses a favourite technique of lengthening the last line of the poem, to emphasise the main point being made by the rest.

Echo

The minutes come, the hours go,
Time passing fast, but leaving slow,
While word-filled patterns soft echo
That time must die tonight.

The people come, the nations go,
Men passing fast, but leaving slow,
While face-filled patterns soft echo
That men must die tonight.

The seasons come, the decades go,
Years passing fast, but leaving slow,
While month-filled patterns soft echo
That years must die tonight.

And Jesus came, and Jesus left,
His words once heard, were later writ;
While Christ-filled patterns softly wept
When Jesus died that night.

And here I sit, and here I stay,
Though all around falls to decay,
While I just watch and softly say,
That something dies each night.

And how I wish to leave this gloom,
To fly up to a higher room,
To catch the echo of the moon
Before I die tonight.

For once in sleep, my mind at rest,
My body dies a death that's blessed,
But oh, how hard I find that quest
To die in sleep each night.

O restless mind, where do you go?
Why do you fly when the flesh is slow?
And why this endless soft echo?
For I must die tonight.

Echo is a sad poem linking death to sleep, a common metaphor used by many poets, including Shakespeare.

For many years, the poet's depression made her wish she would not wake up from sleep. Her depression also made sleep very hard to find, but sleeping tablets only made the problem worse.

She was later to discover that she needed to learn to discipline her thoughts, and to practise replacing negative thoughts with positive ones. Developing this long-term habit helped her control her anger and resentment, two of the many causes of her depression.

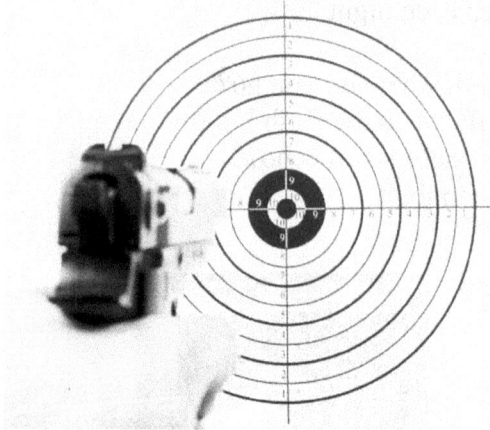

Where is an angry poem, one of relatively few in the poet's collection. It was written while she was recovering in hospital following a serious road accident.

She later came to realise her depression was caused in part by her anger at the world being turned inward against herself, because her upbringing had not allowed her to express her true thoughts.

When anger is not brought out and examined, it can fester in the subconscious and lead to all kinds of destructive behaviours. This poem shows how poorly handled resentments can sometimes result in violence.

Where?   24th November 1977

Where is the world now, hien?
Where is it now?
It bares its teeth at my gate, friend;
It seeks my blood:
That is where it is now.

Where are the friends now, hien?
Where are they now?
They took my money with great promises, friend;
They said they'd help:
That's not what they do now.

Where is that peace now, hien?
Where is it now?
It has never crossed my doorstep, friend;
It never called:
That's what's missing now.

Where are those happy days now, hien?
Where are they now?
They are screwed up in the rubbish bin, friend;
They're chased away:
That's what has gone now.

Where is my gun now, hien?
Where is it now?
It is pointed at the world, friend;
It's aimed to kill:
That's what I'll do now.

Oh, Day of Days   **28th December 1977**

Oh day of days,
How endlessly you stretch –
An infinite path through the universe.
Oh, that I could sleep for a thousand years.

Oh pain of pains,
How cruelly you ache –
Stabs of agony through my wounded heart.
Oh, that I could sleep for a thousand years.

Oh hope of hopes,
How thoughtlessly you flee,
When you are all I have to cling to.
Oh, that I could sleep for a thousand years.

Oh life of lives,
How bitterly you taste!
What can you try to promise me now?
Oh, that I could sleep for a thousand years.

If I Could Take Flight   1977

If I could take flight like a swallow
Oh, how happy I would be,
To wing over mountains and oceans
Further than human eye can see,
But here on the ground I must labour
Where no eye can see me,
Between walls of stone unseen I suffer,
And never will be free.

If stars in these skies turn to diamonds,
They could not clear the price I pay.
Or leaves on these trees turn to sovereigns,
They could not help me fly away.
But still I can dream of tomorrow,
To help me through each day.
Till life and light begin to falter,
And death takes me away.

Section Four

Faith and Recovery

To Face The Sunset was written while the poet was still suffering some of her deepest depressions in life. Sadly, she had to travel a lot further down that road before she took up God's invitation to turn her life around through the 12-Step Program of Recovery.

It was then she learnt, as others have said, God loves us as we are: we do not have to do or be anything to be loved by God. But God loves us too much to let us stay as we are. If we are open to taking up the invitation to follow the road to recovery, God's full power is there behind us, ready to support us whenever we ask.

To Face The Sunset   **9th September 1975**

God, help me walk this rock-strewn path
And guide me so I keep that way,
For in myself there's not enough
To face the sunset at the end of day.

God, help me climb this mountain steep
And guide me so I do not stray
For I alone am far too weak
To face the sunset at the end of day.

God, help me sail this ocean wide
And guide me so I face the fray,
For I have no sure strength inside
To face the sunset at the end of day.

God, help me as I face this world,
And guide me through its ashes grey,
And give me strength, and all I need
To face the sunset at the end of day.

Waiting for the Dawn describes the author's situation as she neared the threshold of recovery.

Two years before the poem was written, a curate had told her about God's unconditional love for her, while she was recovering in hospital after a failed operation.

She accepted God's love for her, and returned to church. A few months later, she handed her will and her life over to God's care, trusting that God could not make any more of a mess of her life than she had. The following spring, she met the person who would lead her to recovery through the 12-Step program.

It was to take another fourteen months after the poem was written, before she came to believe that recovery program could help her as much as it had transformed the lives of others.

Waiting for the Dawn   30th October 1982

An empty wind blows through my mind,
And like the icy blast of death,
The night clings to my aching soul.

I have no certain cause for sorrow,
Though in this mortal body, pain wracked,
I do find some shadows of the past.

God, at least you do not forsake me.
You make these shadows easier to bear,
And send me help when night becomes too dark.

Beyond this darkness, I can trust the dawn,
And sleep can ease, though only for a while;
But when that dawn will be, I cannot say.

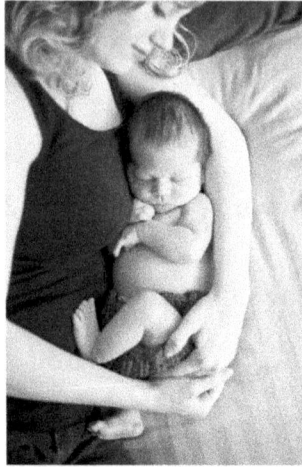

The Quiet Spirit is a poem of consolation in a time of difficulty. It was written about a month after the road accident that put the poet in hospital for a near four-month stay. It was also only a couple of months after the author and her first husband had separated prior to divorce.

Hospital is a notoriously difficult place to sleep because of all the other sick and injured people being cared for in the same ward. To help her get to sleep, Maggie used to cuddle one of the pillows that supported her when she sat up in bed during the day. The pillow's consolation reminded her of her childhood, and those days long ago when a mother's comforting arms would have helped to soothe her.

The Quiet Spirit
6th November 1977

And the quiet spirit,
Resting in its cushioned orb,
Reaches out its balming touch
To ease the sores of life.

Lift me up to mountain heights of old,
Take my hand and give me strength again,
Touch my eyes that I may see once more,
Bathe my ears with music heard before.

For I seek, I struggle like a youth
In fiery passion from distressed ideals;
I chafe at my bonds, I pull my chains
To find a weakness when there's none.

I tremble in untimely fluxion,
Quivering with too youthful an emotion;
I fight against that which cannot be overcome,
So take me back again,

Back to the child's quiet spirit,
Resting in its cushioned orb,
Caressed by balming fingers, easing arms,
Embracing me to find a quiet mind.

Cradle me, Lord   30th September 1981

It is a hard road, this:
Not that I was promised any ease,
But the pain in each footstep weighs me down.
I am getting so tired.

Cradle me, Lord, cradle me:
Say, this too will pass.
Lift me on my feet again:
It's a long, long way that I must go.

It is a cruel world, this:
Not that I was promised any hope;
But the greed in each person weighs me down:
I am getting so tired.

Cradle me, Lord, cradle me:
Say, this too will pass.
Set me in my place again:
It's a long, long war that I must fight.

It is a strange dream, this:
Not that I was promised only grief;
But the love of existence lifts me up:
I am getting renewed.

Cradle me, Lord, cradle me:
Say, Love finds a way.
Help me do your work again:
It's a long, long peace that I go to.

Vision and the Past (II)   13th October 1976

Not to excuse, nor understand,
But to accept.

Not to refute, nor condone,
But to let be.

Not to defy, nor exalt,
But to acknowledge.

Not to reject, nor honour,
But to admit.

Not to destroy nor replace nor condemn
But to trust as an integral part of the past which cannot change.

What it was and what it will be, can never be the same,
But as it was, it is, and will be, must remain.

View of the Sunlight soap factory from
the back of 170 Effra Road in 1972

Sunrise on Doudern Fell was one of the earliest poems the author wrote about the mythical world which came to life in the novel *The Eagle and The Butterfly*. Its unusual metre derives from the melody she heard in her thoughts as she wrote the words.

When Maggie returned from London to live with her parents again after two years as a teenage runaway, her earlier depression returned. She left again in five weeks, but stayed in contact with her parents this time. The window of her small bedsitter in South Wimbledon overlooked the Sunlight Soap Factory (since pulled down for a housing estate).

Her depression lifted once more, and the summer opened up to be one of her best as a young adult.

Sunrise on Doudern Fell   May 1972

It was not day,
Yet already the birds were singing,
And so loud was their chorus
That I awoke.

As sleep left me,
I looked in peace over the landscape,
Which once had been so empty,
And was amazed.

Among the rocks
New grass was quickly springing up,
And the winter-struck forest
Was leafy green.

The beck chattered,
And in its depths I saw new life;
And I thought back – the birds had
Ne'er sung so gay.

And then I knew –
It's the way we look at this old world,
Not the way that it looks back,
That brings the day.

A Christmas Song   1st September 1983

I saw a ship a sailing
With a baby in the prow
And with him Mother Mary
And Joseph in the bow.
And round them flew the angels,
So I asked, 'What do I see?'
They said, 'This is your Saviour:
He has come to set you free.'

I saw a ship a sailing
With some shepherds at the helm;
They sang with jubilation
As they held out a lamb.
And round them flew the angels,
So I asked, 'What do I see?'
They said, 'They give an offering
To the one who'll set you free.'

I saw a ship a sailing
With three wise men in the stern:
They carried gifts and riches,
And above a new star burned.
And round them flew the angels,
So I asked, 'What do I see?'
They said, 'Wise men acknowledge him,
As the king who'll set you free.'

I saw a ship a sailing
With a man nailed to its mast,
And as I asked, 'What has he done?'
The young man breathed his last.
And round him flew the angels,
So I asked, 'What do I see?'
They said, 'The babe became a man
Who died to set you free.'

And I myself am sailing
In this ship that's called the world;
The price I pay to live each day
I give gladly to my Lord.
And round me fly the angels,
Who protect me on life's sea:
The babe, the lamb, the king, the man:
Through his love has set me free.

This traditionally styled carol is a synthesis of the poet's understanding of the Christian message at Christmas.

Shortly after writing it, she joined an interdenominational healing group of Christians who gathered from around the Scottish borders, through the couple who ran the Dundas Galleries in Carlisle at that time. At the healing group, another member introduced her to the 12-Step program of Alcoholics Anonymous as a program of living, not just a way to stop abusing alcohol. This led to the next step in the story of her recovery.

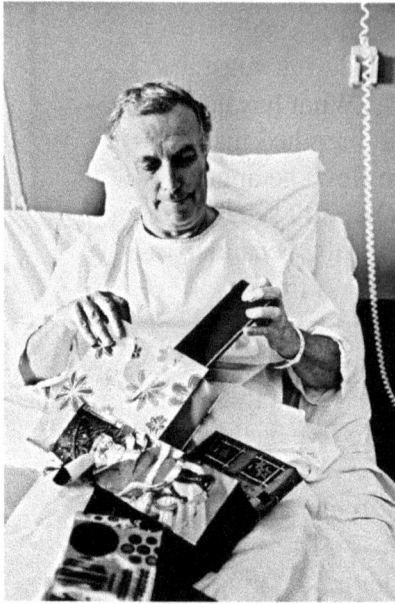

The author wrote *Christmas Prayer* in 1977 as a reflection on Christmas as she lay on traction in a hospital bed with no end in sight to her stay. It has since undergone extensive revisions, in 1982 and in 2021. While the sentiment was powerful, the metre resisted attempts to restrain it.

The first line of verse 5 refers to St Paul's words in 1 Corinthians chapter 9 verse 22: 'I am become all things to all people'. In this, Paul was not advocating that we compromise our beliefs in order to fit in, but that we should use our own gifts and experiences sacrificially to help others we meet, much in the same way that Paul used his qualifications and experience to bring Christianity to the people of his time.

Christmas Prayer 18th December 1977

Christmas Prayer   **18th December 1977**

Lord, still my heart and ease me from my fears:
The winter night is dark: you are its light.
Your star shines down as once it did before,
And brings the promise of a coming dawn.

Christmas music haunts my troubled mind:
I have no gifts to show my gratitude
For all the kindnesses I have received:
I want to give more than a thankful word.

Lord, you know I cannot see the manger,
Tied in this prison of my injured flesh;
But I can still proclaim my alleluias
In thanks for Christ, your gift to save my soul.

Yet, others are blind to your gift of hope:
They cannot see your star that lights the sky.
Although they mark the season, they ignore
The compass that would help them sail their storms.

Lord, help me to be all things to all people:
Let my support sustain their heavy hearts;
Let my joy cheer; my love for you teach them
To see your world of joy which they have lost.

Thus by your grace I too shall give a gift
More precious than the gifts that I receive,
And lose my sorrow for this passing pain
In thoughts of Christ, the greatest gift of all.

The author wrote *Survivor* as she was compiling this volume of poems and starting to prepare the next. It is a synthesis of all she had read as she typed out, edited and commented on her lifetime's poetry.

The poem uses an extended metaphor of a long walk among the Lakeland fells to chart the course of the poet's life. It is interesting to compare it with the similar poem *My Life is Like a Long-Distance Train* (page 31) where while a young adult, she described her life as a train journey over which she had little control. In this poem, written nearly fifty years later, she is clearly in charge of her own fate.

The poem has no distinct rhyming pattern. The meter is fluid, but written to flow. The length of each verse has been deliberately set at two lines less than the verse before. Thus, the past, which people know most, has most detail. The present describes the detail that can be seen, but is more speculative. The future has fewer lines, all speculative. The last verse is deliberately short, summarising the rest of the poem to describe the writer's feelings at that present moment, intensifying the power of the last line.

Survivor

Survivor   **16th December 2021**

Now, as I look down from the plateau of my achievements,
I see the many places I had to conquer:
The steep slopes, the raging rivers, the skidding screes.
I can see too, the resting places: the sheltered lakes,
The wooded slopes, the flower meadows.
And I can see the threading path between them,
Sometimes a deeply rutted track, a paved road,
Or just my own footprints on the dewy turf.

I turn my head towards the heights above me:
Some jagged-toothed; others rounded, lined with trees.
I can hear the call of flowing water –
Perhaps a hidden beck chattering in a forest glade,
A fresh spring bubbling out of the heathered hillside,
Or a quiet tarn above the tree line, nestling in a cwm's embrace.

Tomorrow still calls, tempting me to walk on,
To climb up to new heights, to face new challenges,
To live while life allows with whatever life has left me.
But for now, let me savour the moment of this present.

Here, on this plateau, every moment of that past journey,
Has transformed me into the survivor I am now.

Section Five

Stories

The Cinder Tree 15th January 1988

How many times I've peered through your window
And walked on past your door.
How many times I've followed your shadow,
And still come back for more.
I stand on the edge of sunset,
At the end of time:
A twentieth century reject,
And all I have is rhyme.

I always shook the cinder tree.
Love and wealth are not for me.
We all have our destiny:
Mine's to shake the cinder tree.

How many times I've called out your name –
You turned your back on me!
How many times I've tried to play your game,
And won the cinder tree.
You stand on the edge of dawn,
At the start of day:
Another superhero born
To rise above life's clay.

I always shook the cinder tree.
Love and wealth are not for me.
We all have our destiny:
Mine's to shake the cinder tree.

Do we ever choose the way to go?
Say yes when destiny says no?
And is it right that I who only lose,
Must love what's lost instead of what I choose?

How many times I reached to touch the sky,
And fallen from my stool.
How many times I've asked the question why,
Yet known I was the fool.
I can only live today,
Just this present hour;
Another broken hero felled
By the poison in your flower.

I always shook the cinder tree.
Love and wealth are not for me.
We all have our destiny:
Mine's to shake the cinder tree.

Song to a friend   1982

From dull suburban streets to a city of defeat,
You ran to find a new world and a home;
And some thought you insane when you tried to flee the rain,
They didn't see how much you were alone.
Now we won't meet again cause you took a strange train
Into a land of peace that I still cannot reach;

And now I find you're often on my mind
In many of the things I say and do;
I sit at home and dream alone
As life seems so empty without you.

We used to walk the night away from all the lights
That shone like ropes of diamonds to the sea,
And you unlocked my soul but said I made you whole,
And then we would both dream of being free;
But all our treasured plans slipped away like sand,
When I reached for you one morn to find that you had gone.

And now I find you're often on my mind
In many of the things I say and do;
I sit at home and scheme alone
As life seems so empty without you.

For you ran to escape the storm but found another dawn
When you led our people on to find a day
When you spoke with our voice, voted as our choice
To show convention, there is another way.
But panic struck again, and your supporters ran;
And as we fell to men's hatred, you fell by a vote.

And now I find you're often on my mind
In many of the things I say and do;
I sit at home and sigh alone
As life seems so empty without you.

Many miles away, I watch the fading day.
The lights still shine as they always used to.
Though you have gone, the world still carries on,
Its memory too short to remember you.
A goddess for one year, who took away our fear.
Who taught me how to be,
And showed us a way to be free, truly free.

And now I find you're on my mind
In everything I think and say and do.
I sit at home and cry alone
As everything seems so pointless without you.

A rebel hero with a heart for the poor has always been one of the author's leading motifs. This poem and song was written about one of the characters in her unpublished novel, *The Three Circle Star*, which she wrote while working at the West Cumberland Hospital. The phrase: 'the lights that shone like ropes of diamonds to the sea', describes the lights along the back road to St Bees, on the far side of the valley cradling Whitehaven, which she saw every night shift.

Merry-go-round was written as a song sung by the nightclub singer Isabella Santon, in *Diviner's Nemesis II – Retribution*. She would have sung this song after all the customers had gone home, to vent her cynicism about love and romance. A recording of the song is available from www.eregendal.com.

The author also wrote a short story called *Merry Go Round*. Both works feature in Mark Sheeky's *ArtSwarm* video magazine on YouTube, Series 2 Episode 10, entitled *Children's Games*.

Merry-go-round   15th August 1983

Here's the merry-go-round:
Take your places
For the best show of your life.
First in all the fairground:
See the faces –
Find a husband, find a wife.

All you need for a ticket
Is a heart as cold as ice;
So, take your places,
Break the traces:
Ride to win, and pay the price.

On the merry-go-round?
Don't be frightened:
Put your best mask on and smile.
Others may hit the ground:
You're enlightened;
So leave the inch and take the mile.

If they cry, just ignore it:
That's the way they play the scene.
So, keep on riding;
No confiding:
Love is life, and life is mean.

Dawn

She looks up at me so sadly:
I see the tears in her eyes and my heart reaches out to her –
How can I tell her she has hurt me?

She looks up at me so mischievously:
I see the laughter in her eyes and my past reaches out to her –
How can I tell her she is wrong?

She looks up at me so angrily:
I see the hatred in her eyes and my mind reaches out to her –
How can I tell her it is right?

She looks up at me so trustingly:
I see the acceptance in her eyes
    and my love reaches out to her –
How can I tell her she is safe?

She looks up at me so lovingly:
I see the reflection in her eyes:
    my motherhood reaches out to her –
How can I ask her not to change?

Dawn is a poem about a character in the unpublished novel, *The Three Circle Star*. When she is left alone sleeping in the house by her mother, she is found by the main character Ginny Lee, who identifies with the neglected child and wishes she was in a position to mother her.

I can still remember her   22nd September 1974

I can still remember her,
The light shone through her hair,
Her long dark curly hair:
I still remember her.

I still lie and think of her:
I sigh and she is there,
My saviour from despair –
Oh, I still think of her.

I still live in dreams of her:
Of castles in the air,
A world for us to share –
Oh, I still dream of her.

I can still find tears for her,
For she will never care,
This born love never share:
I'll always love her.

I can still remember her is a poem about a woman seen once in
The Richmond Arms, Hensingham, whose distinctive face and
manner inspired the character Kitty in the novel *The Three Circle
Star*.

The character narrating the poem speaks out of her unrequited
love for the woman described, who has no idea of the castles in the
air being built around her but recognises the infatuation and uses it
to manipulate and control.

My Lady on the White Mare is a poem about the muse Tamara who lived in the High Castle at Halsanger in Berren, in the novel *The Eagle and The Butterfly.*

The longer original poem, written in 1976, was reshaped for the novel when it was published in 2020. The main character Eregendal sings these words from the high window of the ruined castle, pledging continued support to save Tamara, who had been kidnapped by the evil Zoust's flock of jackdaws. When Eregendal voices Zoust's name in the hearing of the wise judge Maredudd, the judge cannot bear to carry the weight of evil associated with the name, and leaves the castle to walk to his death in the nearby river.

The original poem was inspired by a friend who rebelled against the drug treatments she had to endure to control her mental illness.

My Lady on the White Mare   September 2020

My lady upon the white mare,
Robed in white yourself;
With purple orchids in your flaxen hair,
And in your hand a lover's ivy wreath,
And in your eyes a look of wistful care;
Your lips marked by a sorrow worse than death.

My lady, born inspiration,
In its High Castle;
When I returned and brought your father down,
You knew I heralded fair Berren's fall;
The jackdaws took you ere we could be warned
That Halsanger now faced the Last Battle.

My lady, held by caves and bars,
I must seek you now.
I see your proud lands ravaged by this war,
And watch in dread here at your high window
While Zoust's great army gathers from afar.
Now, only you can save us from our foes.

My lady, trapped, who should be free,
I too am fast chained:
Their blood-soaked bonds are now thrown around me:
See how my tired wings are rent and stained.
Yet still I must fight on for what must be,
To bring you to your castle once again.

Visitor is one of the earliest poems about Berren, and became part of the foundation of the novel *The Eagle and The Butterfly*. The character described is a cross between the wizard of Fate, Arzandel, and the religious archetype figure of the Teacher, Ashleigh, both key figures in the story.

Visitor 1971

So like a shadow I saw him,
Standing in the light of the moon;
And as darkness drifted,
He came

To these shores with soft feet
And a message of peace
That warmed my heart.
He sat.

Although I am only a minstrel
Who, having travelled far, rested,
Yet, coming over to me,
He spoke.

Golden words are for God's people:
I myself am not for those;
But such were for me, those lyrics
He sang.

And the wind blew high
Over Doudern Fell in the night,
And the people dreamed of him, as
He left.

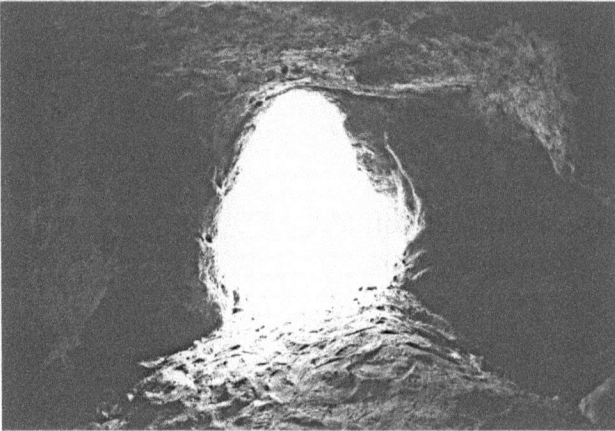

Anthem for the Teacher Ashleigh was written after the first draft of the novel *The Eagle and The Butterfly* was finished, as it was hard for the writer to let go of the character. Here, Ashleigh is described in almost Christlike terms, although in the story he has more affinity with Lazarus.

As the archetype representing religion, Ashleigh's death causes the land to be thrown into the last battle between good and evil.

Anthem for the Teacher Ashleigh   24th November 1976

Ashleigh bore a promise heralded by the prophets;
Ashleigh bore a promise never spoken before.
Ashleigh bore a promise all nations ending:
Ashleigh bore a promise that will stand for evermore.

Ashleigh bore the promise, though the sun was setting,
Ashleigh bore the promise, though the evening came with rain.
Ashleigh bore the promise of the last battle's ending:
Ashleigh bore the promise that we all will rise again.

Petals fall, leaves tremble, the wind changes.
Nor kings nor fools evade the hand of Fate.
Circled time ever parts friends, joins strangers
At the door of life where birth and death wait,
Hand in hand to rest the old, bless the new...
Yet still we cannot measure losing you.

For you bore the promise of the sun's never waning
And you bore the promise of peace for all;
And you bore the promise of happiness reigning,
But Halsanger's happiness will be buried with you.

The Fairy describes an ethereal Tinkerbell-like creature whose enchanted life weaves around our own lives, bringing peace and consolation.

The Fairy

When sunrise dapples on the grassy fields,
And over the hilltops the seagulls weave
Their lonely ways,
She slips into her cloak of elfin green
And take to the misty forests unseen
To greet the day.

When midday fills the vale with summer warmth
And shafts of light dance to the beck's sad laugh,
Its timeless cry,
She drifts across the moorland's empty glades,
Casting petals its waters snatch away,
To say goodbye.

When sunset fingers smudge the seascape red,
And birdsong calls God's creatures to their beds
Another night,
She gathers flowers to scatter on our dreams
And wipes away the tears of unfilled schemes
With smiles of light.

When midnight shrouds the mountains and the sea,
And the cold moon touches the shadowed trees
Across the fells,
She glides by the lake on a silver cloud,
Offering a star in her outstretched hand,
Whispers 'Farewell'.

Section Six

People and Places

On the Road to Bamiyan was inspired by a painting by Heather Bolton RA, following the journey she made from the UK to Pakistan in a mini van.

The poem was originally published in the West Cumberland Arts Co-operative magazine *Raven*.

On the Road to Bamiyan   **18th February 1976**

Echoes from the heights around me in my mind
Descended the depth where I sat, engaged
By stone more ancient than the cloudless sky.

Whispers on the sultry wind caressed my hair
And spoke of pasts I knew but could not place,
In sharp relief behind the starry night.

Moonlight bathed the valley in liquid silver,
Mighty cliffs melted in its ice caress:
Like frozen waterfalls, the long-stilled slopes,

Balm rivers of heaven, coursing down to earth,
Took me skywards with their timeless magic -
Leaving me as stone.

The Clan MacThomas Lament retells some of the stories from the history of the Clan MacThomas of Glenshee and its founding father, McCombie Mhor. While temping as a legal secretary in Perth, the author spent her lunch breaks reading local history in the city library. The studies bore fruit in this song and its companion, *The Fiddler of Glenshee.*

The last line of the second verse refers to a motto carved over McCombie Mhor's hearth at Crandart. The last line of the third verse refers to the clan motto: *Deo Juvante Invidiam Superabo* – with God's help I will overcome envy.

For more information about the Clan MacThomas Society, visit www.clanmacthomas.org.

The Clan MacThomas Lament   September 1997

Farewell, Glenisla, that was our home;
Farewell, Glenshee and the Glascorrie lands.
Our sons are slain by Farquharson's men,
And lawyers' fees stole our living.

Once we were wealthy with cattle and power
In the time of our champion, McCombie Mhor;
But now his hearth at Crandart is cold.
Lord, defend this family.

Farquharson hungered to have what was ours:
He wooed, then spurned fair Elizabeth's hand.
Our feu by right, he stole by decree:
God, help us overcome envy.

Where are you going with your homes on your backs,
Like tinkers travelling these long stony tracks?
We're bound for Deeside, Fife and Lochee.
Gone is the clan of McCombie.

The Fiddler of Glenshee is a companion song to the preceding poem, and has also been performed at several Clan MacThomas gatherings over the years.

Ian Thomson was a famous fiddle player who carved his initials in the main fireplace at the Spittal of Glenshee Hotel. The hotel has since burnt down, leaving the Clan MacThomas without a natural base to stay in the glen. Clan Gatherings now usually meet over the hills in nearby Pitlochry, with excursions to Glenisla and Glenshee.

A little fairy dust has been sprinkled over Ian Thomson's legend, to produce this traditional style folk song.

The Fiddler of Glenshee

Tom's son John, play your fiddle, play your fiddle, man;
Tom's son John, play your fiddle with glee:
Tom's son John, play your fiddle, play your fiddle, man:
Tom's son, the fiddler of Glenshee.

Tom's son John played for Mairi's wedding.
The guests were still dancing all the next day.
The fairies could na sleep for his fiddling:
The dancing stopped when they stole him away.

Tom's son played for the fairies' ceilidh:
Fiddled till Beltaine had come and gone.
The midsummer sun dawned and broke all his fetters –
Tom's son woke up in a wood far from home.

Tom's son John was lost in the forest –
Played his fiddle till the trees had to sway;
Played his fiddle till paths sprung open,
And squirrels and foxes showed him the way.

Ton's son John found the road to the Spittal –
A hundred years he had been away.
Carved his name on a stone in the kitchen,
And Tom's son John is still heard there today.

Tom's son John, play your fiddle, play your fiddle, man;
Tom's son John, play your fiddle with glee:
Tom's son John, play your fiddle, play your fiddle, man:
Tom's son, the fiddler of Glenshee.

FLOWERING

This striking black-and-white photo by the Lithuanian photographer Romualdas Rakauskas, inspired this poem about transience and permanence.

The photographer died in September 2021, shortly before the compilation of this book. His daughter, the artist Eglė Rakauskaitė, continues to keep his memory alive and runs a Facebook page in his name, to illustrate his life and work.

To a Photo by Romualdas Rakauskas   7th May 1975

He held some flowers in his hand.
Mountains sat and watched the world,
Disdaining to observe the man
For whom the glacial rock was hurled.

He held some flowers in his hand.
Fresh petals rivalled leathered cheeks
In colour but not in time's flowing sand
For brilliant hue made grace so weak.

He held some flowers in his hand.
Symbols of transience, not beauty, stood they,
Nodding shyly to the passing wind:
He knows that though they die, he'll stay.

He held some flowers in his hand,
To prove that, though so old, he still could care.
Both he and bloom were bred on the same land,
And in centuries to come, will still nod there.

The author wrote *Remember When* as a reflection about why her great aunt Daisy Johnson never married. Daisy worked as a nurse during the First World War and had been courted by a young man. She never explained what had happened to their relationship.

The poem was originally written to the metre of a popular song tune. Maggie later composed a different tune for it so that she could perform it without infringing on copyright. In performance, she usually sings just the first and last verses.

Remember When   4th August 1983

Remember when you thought me beautiful,
And youth was on my side
In that long hot summer?
Remember when I thought you wonderful,
And life was on your side
In that long hot summer.

A hundred days we shared our pasts and future;
We built our castles in the air.
A hundred hopes lie in ashes in my memory,
For though life goes on, you will nevermore be there.

Remember when your country called for you
And you could not refuse
In that long, hot summer.
Remember when I said I'd wait for you,
But could not say goodbye
In that long, hot summer.

There are no ties, and nothing to recall you,
Yet still you live while I can dream.
A distant cross for a soldier of misfortune,
And an empty life for the woman of his dreams.

End of the conversation – revisited   23rd January 2002

Please try to listen to me more.
Don't try to change me quite so much.
I don't need you to try to fix my life for me:
I'd just like to be understood.

My opinions are as valid as
Your opinions are as valid as
My opinions are as valid as
Your opinions are valid.

This unusual poem was written after having an unsatisfactory conversation with a friend. One of the author's limitations as an autist is that she does not fully process conversations until after they have finished, leaving a lot unsaid. It can be hard to set and maintain personal boundaries when one does not realise until later that one's personal boundaries have been breached.

The circular second verse emphasises the need for us to respect each other's autonomy, and not to try to control one another because we think we know best.

Landscape 3rd December 1977

I am an island with shallow shores.
If your boat can't sail into my bay,
Do not blame me
For I cannot shift my sands.

I am a cloud blown by the wind.
If your kite can't catch up with my flight,
Do not blame me
For I cannot control the wind.

I am an ocean.
If your country does not border on my beaches,
Do not blame me
For I cannot move mountains –
As quickly as you want me to.

Landscape is a poem about a friendship where one of the people involved wants more than the other person is able to give. Once again, the message is couched in terms of physical places and objects.

The Feral Kitten was written in response to a news story about a couple who found an abandoned and starving wildcat kitten while travelling in the Highlands of Scotland. They took it to an animal rescue centre to recover.

The Feral Kitten   **14th November 2020**

I bend and curl,
Poised, ready to strike;
Wary of the hand that reached,
Frightened in my vulnerability.

I have nothing but my spirit.
Weak and hungry, still I fight
Against the blanket's warmth,
The reassuring hand stroke,
The gentle voice.

Until, pressed against another's warmth,
I feel a heartbeat rhythm through my fur,
And turn to a familiar smell,
To knead the flesh and suckle once again.

In 2021, the author took part in the Writing East Midlands *Beyond The Spectrum* writing course. The following series of haikus describing her experiences of lockdown during the Covid-19 pandemic, was written as one of the skill-extending exercises set by the course leaders.

Lockdown Haikus   8th February 2021

Beyond my window,
Children skip and run to school.
I stay locked at home.

A blank calendar:
No more trips out to meetings,
But plenty of Zooms.

Being so busy,
I look out at the garden
And envy the grass.

Disinfect the post,
Hide behind the mask and gloves –
Oh, for just one hug.

In my home's prison,
Daily routine gives structure.
What price, my freedom?

Section Seven

Humour

He said that he'd seen Oval
sailing out to sea

An image from the cartoon video created in 2019

The author volunteered to be Minutes Secretary for several local groups when younger, and sometimes found it rather frustrating. After one particularly challenging meeting, she wrote the poem *The Shape of Things*. In 2019, she created a simple cartoon video to illustrate her narration. This was first aired in Mark Sheeky's video magazine *ArtSwarm* on YouTube, Series 2 Episode 4: *Curves* (from about 10 minutes).

The poem is an observation of prejudice in a culturally closed community, describing how some people need to have a person to pick on to flatter their own egos.

The Shape of Things   30th June 1976

The Squares and the Triangles were having a debate
About those nasty circles, when Rectangle came in late.
He said that he'd seen Oval
Sailing out to sea,
While I took the meeting minutes,
And it seems like they took me.

Young Oblong was dissatisfied – he raised his fist up high,
While old many-sided Polygon gave a little sigh –
'You won't catch up with Oval:
He said he would get free.'
And I took those meeting minutes,
And I could swear that they took me.

The most acute Triangle said it wasn't fair,
When in walked a passing Rhomboid, invited by a Square.
He said that of that Oval,
'Twas the last that we would see;
And I ate some meeting minutes,
And the hours ate up me.

Eventually Pentangle stood up: he was most annoyed:
'We need to have an Oval, you stupid old Rhomboid!
Without curved shapes around us,
Our straightness we can't see!'
So they called me Hyperbola
And began to pick on me.

The curious poem *Plastic* grew out of the author's concern about consumerism and the need for many of us to make a living doing a job we do not believe in.

The poem includes several contemporary references from the 1970s: Andy Warhol's gaudy portraits of Man Ray and Bridgit Bardot; Scott Joplin, whose rag time piano pieces were popularised by Joshua Rifkin in 1973; and the David Essex hit *Gonna Make You A Star*.

Plastic

Take three queens off to strawberry pie
To see the popstars high in the sky
Which one says he'll make me by and by!
This is the world, and where am I?
It's a sham.

Take Scott Joplin's ragtime, beaten well,
Add an ounce of Andy Warhol's Hell,
Throw in a couple of Party spells…
This is the world, which I must sell!
It's a sham.

Dig up a book by an unknown great,
Time entrance to be politely late,
Rip out the guts of those whom you hate.
This is the world, my house of fate!
It's a sham.

I am your salesman, and naught ails me,
Except the want of serenity,
Except the endless need to be free.
This is the world, its price I see:
It's a sham.

You pay the price and you take the wares,
So shut out that growing howl of despair.
Do not forget that you must not share!
This is the world, for whom I care…
I'm a sham.

Ode to a Nairn Ginger Oat Biscuit was written as another exercise during the Writing East Midlands *Beyond The Spectrum* writing course in 2021. When participants were asked to write an ode about a favourite food, Maggie chose ginger oatcakes. Other students enjoyed the poem so much, they encouraged her to record it and post it on YouTube and Facebook.

Nairn's wrote back and thanked Maggie for posting the poem in praise of their product.

Ode to a Nairn Ginger Oat Biscuit   26th January 2021

Oh, just an oatcake in my hand;
But so much more – a taste so grand
With sugar sweet and ginger spicy:
Better than foods twice as pricey.

I love to eat you with my tea,
A fitting treat to follow meat;
I love to eat you with my supper,
A scrummy snack with yummy cuppa.

Others sing of haggis tasty;
I will praise my wee oat cakie;
And give thanks for Nairn's good brand
That makes this product in Scotland.

In 1972, the author worked as a temporary clerk, helping to combine two artwork systems after Kays Cards merged with Forget Me Not Cards. She spent an interesting summer filing poems and captions with three other colleagues.

Among the papers were several well-crafted inspirational poems written by a highly regarded poet, composed to comfort people in times of tribulation and to help people celebrate in times of joy.

During lunch breaks, Maggie wrote several greetings cards spoofs, and could not let this writer's work pass without at least one gentle lampoon.

A Poem by Impatience Weak   Summer 1972

My, how the years
    They come and go
With summer sun
    And winter snow.

And yet, as you grow up
    with the trees
You find that every
    Season's breeze

Bears tears and joys,
    Hurts and fun
Like changing seasons,
    One by one.

But don't despair
    Now you're getting old.
You'll still survive
    The winter's cold.

And with the new day
    Every morn
You'll walk through Life's
    Great fields of corn!

And to finish, *Silly Song*, a poem about dissatisfaction. Perhaps the grass is not always greener on the other side.

Silly Song   Spring 1971

Silly footsteps walking over
Silly little mountain ranges:
Silly words I speak to
Silly strangers.

Silly lessons that they teach me in
Silly places called colleges and schools:
Silly words are what I'm taught by
Silly fools.

Silly, silly, silly, silly!
Silly world that I can't bend!
How I long to be out of silly, living with
Stupid men.

About the Author

Former teenage runaway Maggie Shaw found her life turned around through a chance meeting at Ennerdale in 1980. After a spiritual transformation, Maggie became a Mental Health Dietitian and studied Divinity at Edinburgh. When she retired in 2018, Maggie began publishing her back catalogue of novels and songs.

Maggie's past inspires her fast-paced yet deep adventure novels, with six published through Eregendal to date: *The Vision and Beyond* (2018), *Diviner's Nemesis I: Avenger* (2019), *Diviner's Nemesis II – Retribution* (2020), *The Eagle and The Butterfly* (2020), *The Last Thursday Ritual in Little Piddlington (2021),* and *The Eagle and The Raven* (2021). Maggie's next novel is due out in 2022.

Cheshire-based Maggie is also a church musician and songwriter, with music and articles published online, in magazines, and through the local press and radio.

Index of Poems

Index of Poems - continued